Custom Curves

Karen McTavish

on-word bound books

publishing & media

Duluth, Minnesota

This book is dedicated to Ronda K. Beyer,
honoring the lives of her son, Darrell,
and her brother, Arden.

CUSTOM CURVES Copyright © 2011 by Karen McTavish. All rights reserved.

Copyright use and this Book

The purchaser has the right to use any of these patterns repeatedly for personal use or in a custom quilting business. This grant does not extend to having the patterns entered into a digital, computerized automated quilting machine without the express written consent of the Author and the Publisher. You can purchase digitized versions of these patterns. Check www.designerquilts.com for more information. Anyone wishing to use any design for advertisement or any other publication must receive written consent of the Author and Publisher. The purchaser may not copy or distribute these patterns for monetary gain.

No part of the accompanying DVD may be reproduced or utilized in any form or by any means, electronic or mechanical, without permission in writing from the Publisher.

Photo Credits:
Karen's bio pic: Alyssa Olson / Duluth, MN / aolson@uwsuper.edu
Ronda's bio pic: Supplied by Ronda K. Beyer / Tualitin, OR
Cover and all other photos: On-Word Bound Books / Duluth, MN

Printed in China by C & C Offset Printing.

DVD replicated in China by C & C Offset Printing.

Published by On-Word Bound Books LLC. / 803 East 5th St./ Duluth, Minnesota 55805
http:/www.onwordboundbooks.com/

ISBN13 978-0-9744706-6-5

10 9 8 7 6 5 4 3 2 1

Table of Contents

Introduction

Inspiration and creativity come in many forms. Long ago, quilting guild members would pass down original, hand-made quilting designs to other members. Throughout the years, sharing these original patterns within the guild sometimes created a style uniquely their own.

When I first started quilting, *meandering* was all the rage for machine quilters. *Micro-stippling* became popular shortly thereafter. And finally, *McTavishing* became the favorite background filler. I suppose *McTavishing* will change into something else one day too.

Like most things in quilting, new techniques evolve, and changes morph and shape our level of creativity. Today, there is a new take on the popular, traditional background filler, crosshatching. Traditional straight-line crosshatching is still effectively used in today's quilts but now there is a new twist: curved crosshatching.

Ronda Beyer is the undisputed expert on curved crosshatching so I have invited her to my studio to help us all learn the ins and outs of this exciting new technique.

This book and DVD combine my copyright-free patterns with Ronda's expertise in curved crosshatching. This combo is an excellent visual aide, allowing you to figure out the mysteries of curved crosshatching. ෨

Review

I already talked about how to use pattern motifs, or *elements*, in my previous pattern book, *The Secrets of Elemental Quilting*. But, for folks who haven't seen that book, I'll do a short review before we get started.

Each quilting motif in this book is designed as an element. By combining an element in many different ways you will come up with a unique design with elegant continuity. For example, you can mirror an element multiple times to design a block, or place an element end-to-end to create a border.

Of course the designs in this book are pretty small for a quilt top so you will have to resize them in order to use the motif. You can take the design to a copy center for enlargement or reduction. Make several different copies, enlarging or reducing by percentages. For example, I might enlarge a design by 30%, 50% and 75%, then take it home, audition each size, and figure out which one works in my quilt.

When the design is the right size it's easy to transfer it to the quilt by marking directly on the fabric, using a light box or transferring the design from the back of the quilt.

The motifs from *The Secrets of Elemental Quilting* and from *Custom Curves* are available from a number of different digital design retailers. Visit my website, www.designerquilts.com, for direct links to my digitized patterns.

If you like to create your own patterns you can start with a piece of paper and a pencil. Play with lines and swirls until you see a motif come together and you are happy with your design.

Making a quilting design decision can only be done by auditioning several designs against the quilt top. Your gut will tell you if it works or doesn't work.

Once you pick your main motif, work other elements of the design into the quilt top too. You can use the same element combined in new ways and in new places: in the center blocks, on-point blocks and corners. The design, if slightly altered and added to, will also look great incorporated in the border.

Remember, do the hardest thing and push yourself – it always pays off in the end. ℰℷ

Supplies

To make registration marks on your quilt top, you will need to use safe marking tools. Some products which both Ronda and I have found to be safe are the air erasable purple pens which will disappear in 24 hours, chalk pencils which will require you to remove the markings with a damp sponge after quilting, and blue water soluble pens which will require you to remove the markings by submerging the quilt completely in water.

All three of these methods of marking are based on the color of your quilt surface. If you have a purple quilt top for example, you can't use the purple air erasable pen because you wouldn't be able to see the markings. You may want to use the chalk pencil instead in a white or gray color.

Generally you can find these marking products at your local quilt shop or at large fabric chain stores. Chalk pencils can also be found at fine art supplies stores under "pastel pencils." Choose light gray or white and handle with care so the chalk doesn't break.

The tool I like to use for "un-marking" is the Clover eraser pen. This is great for removing mistakes made by the blue water soluble pen or purple air erase pen. It completely removes the pen marks so you can re-draw your design without having to spray water on the area. ℰℷ

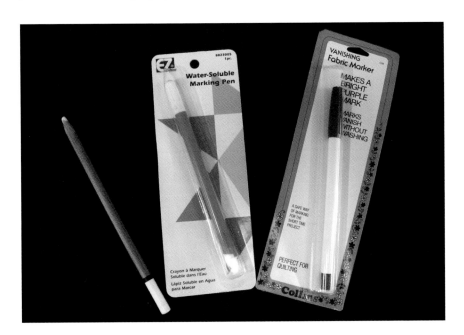

Creating Curved Crosshatching

Before you start your curved crosshatching you will want to create a large plus sign in your quilting space. See how the design below has straight lines going down the center of the motif and across the middle? Draw these registration lines with your Omnigrid ruler and your favorite marking tool such as the purple air erasable pen, chalk pencil, or blue water soluble pen. If you are choosing to mark all of your curved crosshatching before you quilt, you would need to do all the markings on a flat surface, such as a table. Once your registration lines are drawn, you are ready to begin drawing the curved crosshatching lines. Ronda is using the largest ruler available in her *Ronda's Rulers* set called the "Double S" large ruler. For larger motifs, such as this one, you will want to use the largest ruler, but for smaller motifs you can use smaller rulers in her set such as the "Double S" medium ruler.

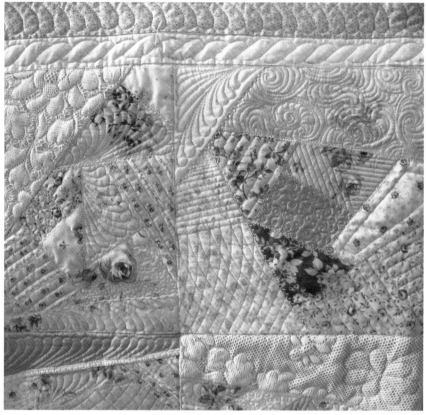

Place the ruler on the motif with the "hill" facing away from your belly. Imagine you are pregnant; that is the curve placement of your ruler. Move the ruler until it meets the lines of the "+" sign, making sure your ruler touches both the vertical and the horizontal registration lines, as shown. Mark the curve with your marking pen. Make a decision now – do you want ¼ inch, ½ inch, or larger curved crosshatching? Ronda recommends keeping it small: ¼ inch to ½ inch is best. Look for the lines on the ruler. These etchings will help you line up your curved crosshatching. Continue to mark your lines by moving your ruler across the motif in one direction, diagonally. Watch the enclosed DVD to help you better understand this marking process.

This is what the end stage of the marking process looks like (right). Don't forget, there is a "belly" that will appear at the top of each curve as you mark. As you mark, you will think that the curved crosshatching is not coming out perfectly. But if you keep marking from the starting point of the registration line to the ending point of the other registration line, ignoring the "belly," you can't mess this up. This is the beauty of curved crosshatching. No matter what you are thinking, you have to trust the process.

Adding a frame around your curved crosshatching gives you more freedom to place crosshatching in any space in your quilt. In smaller blocks to random spaces, the sky's the limit! But first you will need registrations marks (the "+" sign) and then you will need to create the frame. To start your frame, place the "Crescent Moon" large ruler down on

your motif or quilting space. Mark your diamond grid frame by creating four lines. To create a solid frame you will need to double your lines. Using the "Crescent Moon" large ruler, repeat your first frame lines but this time, push your ruler up ¼ inch. This will give you a ¼ inch diamond frame with the appearance of cording. Framing will showcase your curved crosshatching wherever you place it.

After making the frame, you can mark the curved crosshatching in the motif, as shown below. To create the basket weave effect, the curved crosshatching is marked with the "Crescent Moon" ruler using alternating ¼ inch and ½ inch spacing. With the marking pen we've simulated micro-stippling. This is a great way to make your curved crosshatching even more eye-catching. Imagine this with a delicate gold metallic thread.

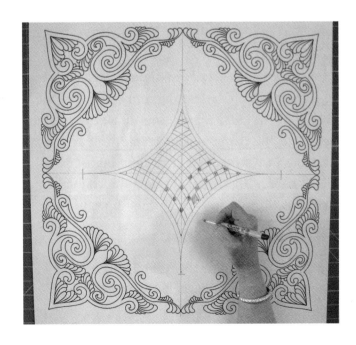

To practice your curved crosshatching, get yourself a small bit of fabric and draw your registration lines with your Omnigrid ruler, creating a large "+" sign. Push your "Crescent Moon" large ruler to the registration lines with the "belly" towards the center "plus" as shown. Now mark your curve on your fabric using your air erasable pen.

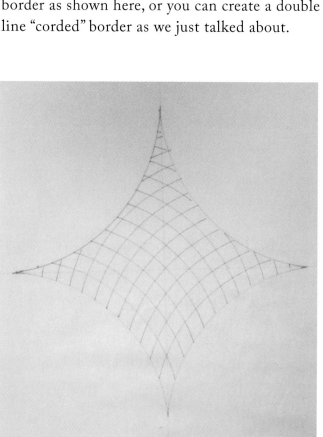

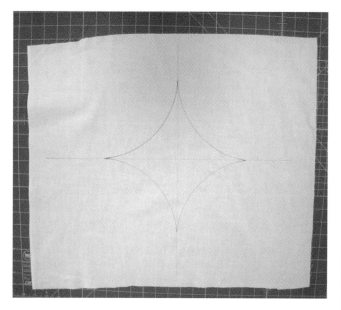

Repeat this marking on all four sides to create this shape (right). You can create a single line border as shown here, or you can create a double line "corded" border as we just talked about.

To mark your curved crosshatching, use the "Crescent Moon" large ruler and start with the "belly" of the ruler mimicking the shape of your belly and the curve of your frame. You may start drawing in your curved crosshatching lines on either side of the frame. Follow the frame in two directions, using the etching lines to help you mark evenly.

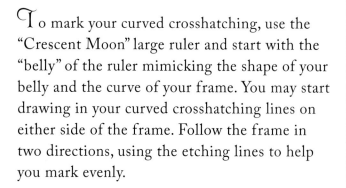

On the DVD, I quilt this sample on a domestic machine. Have a look there for more details.

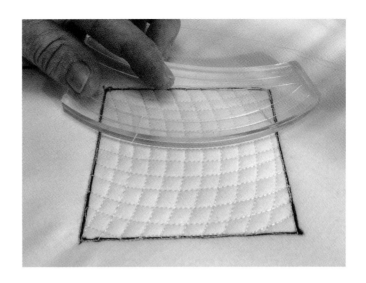

This photo is showing the etching lines in the ruler: visual aids to help you keep your hopping foot ¼ inch to ½ an inch from each quilting line. Once you start quilting, you can see that if you line up the quilting line with the hopping foot, you can trust your hopping foot to do all the measuring work for you.

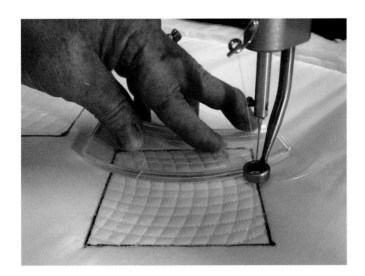

We are "sneaking" up the side of the ditch to get to the lines that are hiding in the corners. Some lines, such as lines in the corners, will be difficult to get to at the end of your block. Traveling via stitching in the ditch will help you finish your curved crosshatching.

It is very easy to create curved crosshatching on the longarm when you use your ruler as a guide. This is the final result of using Ronda's smallest ruler in her set – it's the plop, drop and quilt method with no marking.

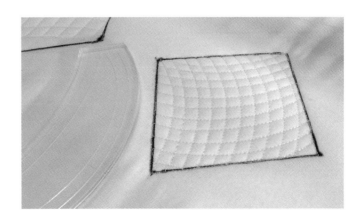

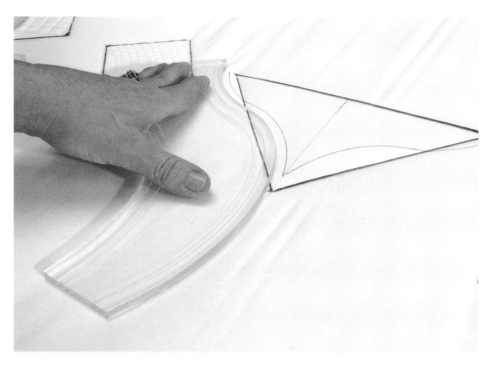

To quilt on-point blocks such as this design, draw a registration line in the middle of the triangle using an air erasable pen. Next, find the natural belly of the curve in the "Double S" medium ruler and place the ruler down on the fabric. Try out different ruler orientations until you are pleased with the curve and then mark your curved crosshatching registration lines. Flip the ruler to create the same line on the opposite side. To create the double line "corded" frame, drop the ruler down ¼ or ½ inch from the first drawn line and repeat your frame lines on both sides.

Using the same ruler, draw out your curved crosshatching as described previously, or quilt using the no-mark method. Notice how the micro-stippling is added here to create more texture in the curved crosshatching.

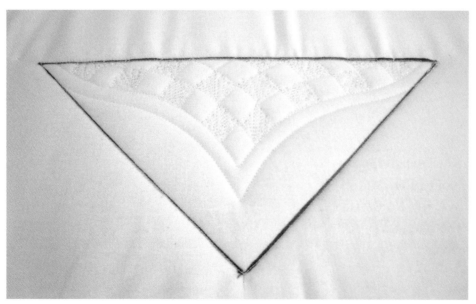

To create the cathedral window you will need the "Crescent Moon" large ruler. To start, draw your registration lines of your block, find the center of the block and mark a dot in the center of the top registration line with an air erasable pen. This is your registration reference to create the cathedral frame. Slant your "Crescent Moon" ruler to the side, and mark your cathedral window frame from the corner of your block to the center dot on the top line. You can double mark your curved line to create a ¼ inch double line frame. Repeat on the other side. Echo your window frame to create your crosshatching.

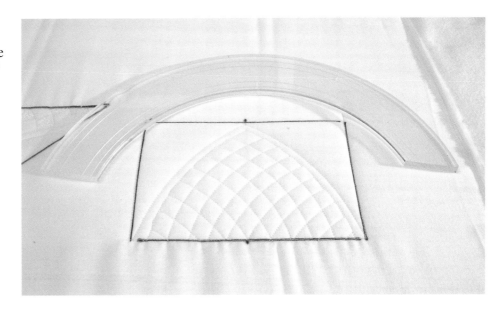

In this square block we used a single line to frame the curved crosshatching. I wanted you to see the difference it makes using two lines for a frame, as shown above in the cathedral window and opposite in the on-point design, versus one single line for a frame, as shown on the left.

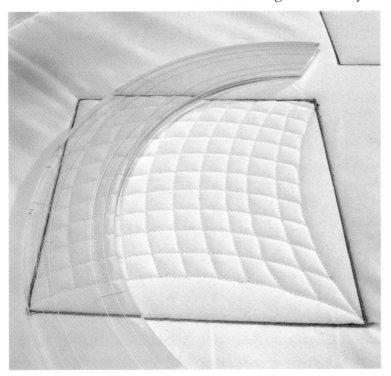

No matter which style of curved crosshatching you like, give yourself permission to play around with it. Experiment and have fun. Be sure to watch the DVD for more instruction on how to achieve this beautiful style of quilting. ❧

Stars for Arden
(92" x 92")

I had planned to make a black and tan quilt for my brother's new home. Instead, it ended up being a memorial/tribute quilt for him. In June 2006 my brother left this world in his own way. This quilt helped me through my journey of grief. Many tears were shed while creating this quilt. I used Home Dec cotton chintz and cotton sateen (which are heavier fabrics) and incorporated a toile print to showcase my love of fiber, and my brother's love of these colors and of toile fabrics. I commissioned the embroidered block centers through ebay.

My brother and I shared a love of the beauty of the outdoors and of gardens which I incorporated in my quilting motifs: a little bit masculine and not *too* fancy. This was my first adventure in curved crosshatching and I learned many lessons on creating this style of quilting. I also added some crystals to give a touch of light to this quilt that I found at times very dark.

I wanted to create something that would keep his memory alive and to help me survive this life altering loss, but mostly to make him proud of his Sis. ~ *Ronda K. Beyer*

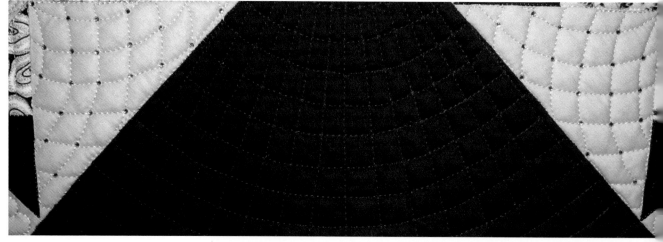

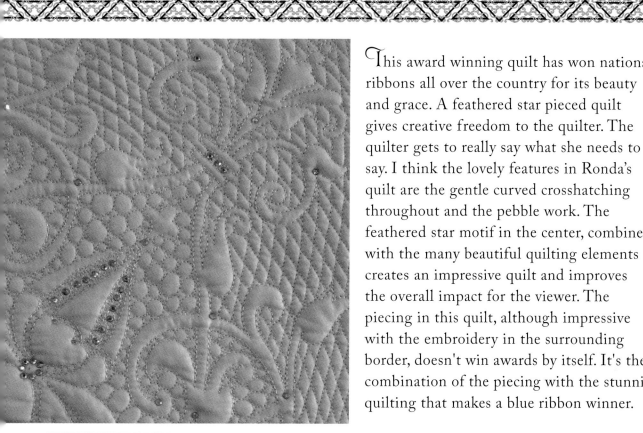

This award winning quilt has won national ribbons all over the country for its beauty and grace. A feathered star pieced quilt gives creative freedom to the quilter. The quilter gets to really say what she needs to say. I think the lovely features in Ronda's quilt are the gentle curved crosshatching throughout and the pebble work. The feathered star motif in the center, combined with the many beautiful quilting elements creates an impressive quilt and improves the overall impact for the viewer. The piecing in this quilt, although impressive with the embroidery in the surrounding border, doesn't win awards by itself. It's the combination of the piecing with the stunning quilting that makes a blue ribbon winner.

Royal Icing
(64" x 64")

Royal Icing started out with my colors, aqua and red. I seem to be drawn to green and wanted to make a quilt that showcased these subtle colors. I used one of my favorite fibers for hand appliqué: ultra suede – no need to turn raw edges and my stitches melt into it like butter. My damask quilting design gave it the feel of a lovely cake, thus the name, Royal Icing. I incorporated my curved crosshatching, love of rope border quilting, and feathers. I love scallop borders; they take a bit more time but are so worth it. ~ *Ronda K. Beyer*

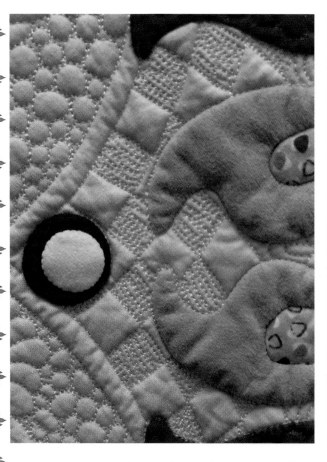

I once had to judge one of Ronda's quilts at the NW Quilting Expo before I knew Ronda personally. And I didn't know who had made the quilt when I had judged it. When I saw the quilt, I knew it would be in the running for Best of Show. There are some quilts that scream at you when you are in the judging room, "Here I am! I am your Best of Show!" And sure enough, after hours of judging with another judge and our scribes, we had our winner. It was a deserved Best of Show. *Royal Icing*, which looks very much like the quilt I once judged, has won many national awards around the country. This quilt is the "perfect storm" for a competition quilt – appliqué with expert machine quilting design and construction. These techniques need to be done with mastery in their craft to achieve the awards that have been bestowed on this quilt.

Blocks

A block might seem like a big, square, empty canvas. It can be easier to design a block if we think of it as two triangles (a square block split in half). Using a registration line we can "cut" the block in half. It is very easy on the eye to place two mirror image designs in the space. This gives the block energy, flow and nice symmetry. Read about my technique for mirror imaging in the On-Point pattern section.

Victorian Peacock

This pattern easily
doubles and quadruples
to make larger blocks,
on-point designs, corners,
borders, and frames.

This shows the
pattern doubled and
then arranged in
four on-point sets
to create a frame.

This border uses a doubled pattern as well. The
doubled on-point motif is set right side up and
upside down, one after another, to create a border.

This pattern uses a single motif, repeated four times to create a frame.

This border is the same as the previous one, but it shows how to join the corners to create a continuous border.

These on-point blocks show two different ways of using the doubled motif in repetition to create a new and exciting bigger block. Either of these two patterns could be used as a wholecloth centerpiece.

This pattern is the same as the previous page's on-point design (lower right), but it has been turned 90 degrees. You could use this pattern as a small wholecloth design or to fill in some plain space in any other quilt.

Requiem for a Botanical

This 3-part pattern is perfect for filling in a square-within-a-square block, but the pattern is easy to separate into its components too, as shown below, giving you many more options.

Here are a few fun ways to use the smaller seashell and scroll: large block, small block and a border.

You can easily make a pretty block filler by reflecting and repeating the main element four times. Of course you could also do the same thing as shown previously and pull elements of the motif apart to create your own pattern.

Here is an another example of using the entire motif to create a block filler. This time, the larger seashells are on the inside and the smaller ones are on the outside.

Excogitate

In this pattern, I am showing one way to design a block.
Draw (or imagine) a quadrant. Then play around with lines
and shapes until you figure out a pattern you like and that can
be reflected in a pleasing manner. Draw in one corner of your
block and then to finish the pattern, simply reflect and repeat.

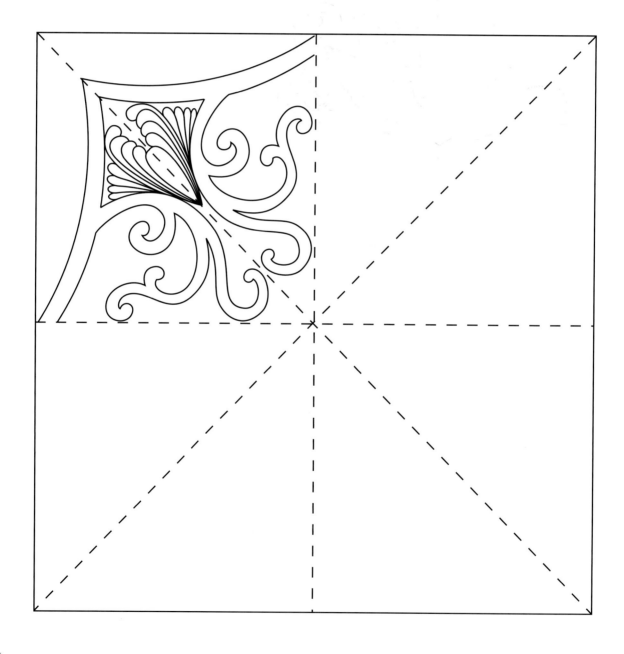

Here's what the pattern looks like once it has been reflected and repeated to each quadrant.

And here is the pattern with a slight modification - I took away the feathers. You can add or take away any part of an element in your motifs too. Go nuts!

Dee-Vine

This pattern is relatively easy to create a block with by reflecting and repeating. You can draw in a quadrant or just play with placement until you are happy.

Reflecting this pattern with the feathers oriented to the outside makes a nice two part small block.

Reflecting with the feathers facing each other makes a larger block (right) or an on-point corner design (below).

Reflecting and repeating your on-point corner design can give you an elaborate block.

Reorienting your two part block and repeating it four times, reveals yet another beautiful block.

A simple frame can be made by using the element four times, leaving open space in the center.

A more elaborate frame can be made by using the on-point corner design four times, leaving open space in the center.

Tribal Block

ℑ drew one quarter of this pattern and then reflected it to get the overall pattern - which I really like. But I can't figure out what else to do with this one besides use it as a block. If you come up with something, send me a picture.

Quintessence

Here's another example of drawing in part of a pattern with plans to use it muliple times to finsh the block.

You can make a few different styles of blocks with this element too.

Try turning your motif in all different directions to create new patterns.

This pattern works well for creating a frame or border.

Lotus Bloom

I drew one flower and then reflected it to get this small block.

Turning the flower block's points in, gives you one block option. And turning the points out, gives you another.

Ornament

This pattern reminds me of a spade on a playing card but also looks like an ornament you would hang from a christmas tree.

Wouldn't these patterns
make beautiful cookies?

Tri-Heart Scrollwork

Here's a great design for a circle block. Again, I drew one portion of this pattern and then reflected it to get the overall pattern - which is shown on the next page.

Above is the finished pattern, and to the right is a frame variation. Here you can either showcase something already existing in your quilt or you can add another quilting element in the center.

This pattern also lends itself well to a rectangular block, or to being turned into a border. There are two border variations here. Below, you'll see a single motif border and to the right you'll see a double motif variant.

Victorian Swan

Here's another great design for a circle block. Again, I drew one portion of this pattern and then reflected it to get the overall pattern.

Here's the overall pattern. See how great it fits in a circle block? Of course you can use it in a square block too.

This is a funny thing. This pattern is the exact same as the pattern above. All I did was turn it 45 degrees. But look how different it looks. Remember to audition your motifs in all kinds of ways: different angles, different sizes and different combinations. You never know what is going to look the best.

This pattern can also be turned into a frame, as seen above, or into a funky border: single, as seen right, or double, as seen below.

On-point

Seussian Swirl

When working with on-point designs you will need to learn to use a reflection, or mirror image, of the pattern. You will need white paper and a black Sharpie pen. Make a copy of the pattern, to your size specifications, on white paper. Flip the paper over and trace the image from the back with your Sharpie. Now you have your mirror image. This can be used just like a plastic stencil for marking a quilt top. If your fabric is dark you will need a light box to see your pattern, but if your fabric is light you should be able to see through the fabric to trace the pattern with your blue water soluble pen or chalk pastel pencil. Using purple air erasable pen is not an option for this process as the pen markings only last twenty-four hours.

This pattern easily doubles and quadruples to make larger blocks, on-point designs, corners, borders, and frames.

Points in, repeated
four times, creates a
beautiful celtic knot
inspired block filler.

This frame uses
a single motif,
repeated four times.

Toruk

These on-point blocks show two different ways of using the motif in repetition to create a new and bigger design. Either of these two patterns could be used as a wholecloth centerpiece.

This pattern uses the main motif turned at a forty-five degree angle and then repeated four times to create an on-point design.

This frame uses a single motif, repeated four times. You could turn this frame forty-five degrees for another variation.

This pattern uses a variation on the frame from the previous page and the four part block. You could use this pattern as a small wholecloth design or to fill in some plain space in any other quilt.

Cerebellum

Y̶ou can use this element in an on-point design by itself by taking the open ended scroll right to a seam edge, as shown in the first drawing, or you can easily reflect the pattern to make a larger on-point block, as shown above. This element also lends itself well to making a very fancy border or frame.

Putting together your doubled motif in different ways can create blocks with very different centers.

Kirpan

Here's what the pattern looks like once it has been reflected and repeated with the points towards eachother.

And here I've reflected and repeated with the points away from each other.

Both of these blocks were made by repeating the doubled pattern (previous page) four times: one time points in, the other, points out.

Feel free to get creative and make your own frame. See the two different options shown here? I bet you can come up with another.

Taj Mahal

An elegant block can be made by repeating the element four times with the points facing in. If you want the points to touch in the middle you'll have to "nudge" the design a bit, shortening the outer edges. A border or frame can be made by alternating the motif, point up and then point down, nestling the on-point design into a continuous scroll and feather frame.

A pleasing frame can be made by using the element four times, touching the outermost feather tips together and facing the points out. This will leave you with enough space in the middle to quilt a centerpiece or frame an appliqué block.

I've placed a simple block in the center which I created by reflecting the motif. I think this could make a nice wholecloth design. What if you placed the border from the previous page around the outside of your wholecloth as a frame? If anyone does this, please send me picture.

Stealth On-Point

Here's another example of drawing in part of a pattern and then reflecting it to create the finished product, which you see below.

It's easy to make a another on-point motif by reflecting your original element.

This pattern works well for creating a frame or border around a block.

 A flowing scrollwork block can be made by repeating the element
four times with the points facing in. If you want the points to touch
in the middle you'll have to "nudge" the design a bit, shortening the
outer edges. You can also leave more space in the middle, creating a
star patterned center (not shown). A border or frame can be made by
alternating the motif, point up and then point down, nestling the on-
point design into a continuous scrollwork frame.

Rapture

Reflecting this motif along the long side of the pattern gives you a symetrical, vase shaped design.

A flowing scrollwork border or frame can be made by alternating the motif, point up and then point down, nestling the on-point design into a continuous scrollwork motif.

Using the motif twice on the previous page created a symmetrical vase shaped pattern. But here, I am showing how to create an asymmetrical pattern. Simply reflect the motif and then flip your reflection so that you do not have symmetry. It might seem odd, but in this case it works well.

No matter if you use symmetry or asymmetry, this motif creates a flowing pattern that is easy on the eyes.

Any one of this chapter's on-point designs could be used on a pin-wheel patterned pieced quilt as shown below.

Water Lily Scroll

This is a hugely versatile pattern. Check out all the options. I bet you can come up with even more.

Reflect the motif once and you come up with a well-proportioned on-point pattern. Lay the elements out end to end and you come up with fun border.

Here I've quadrupled the pattern seen on the previous page to make a more complex block.

This is really the same design as above, but I've oriented the leaves and flowers to the outside and the scrolls to the inside to make a new block.

This frame and the corner below are the building blocks for the complex wholecloth pattern on the next page. Starting with this frame, I added a single motif to each "empty" spot on the top, bottom, right and left. Then, I added the corner that you see below. I created another smaller frame to fit inside the outer, elaborate frame, and then finished off the design by adding the first block we made with this motif as a centerpiece.

Try out this pattern as a wholecloth if you want. Or you can break down the component parts and use them individually: outer frame, corner, inner frame, centerpiece, or single motif.

Borders & Sashing

The toughest thing about borders and sashing are the corners. This is your challenge. When you are looking at a quilt, your eye will always fall to the corners. You must make sure your corners are all the same. How do you do this? First, pick your design. Audition a few different designs under your quilt border corner. Notice the shape that the corner is making. Is it flattering? Can you "nudge" it or modify it into a corner motif? Use the mirror image for your opposite corner. Most of the time, you will have to do some custom hand-drawing for your corners.

Floral Flair Scroll

ℑ'm showing you three different things with these examples.

1) I'm showing how you can turn a corner with a sashing pattern by adding a small corner element.

2) This sashing motif easily doubles and quadruples to make longer borders or frames.

3) You can make continuous scrollwork to join one section of sashing to another.

1.

2.

3.

2.

3.

Hook & Line

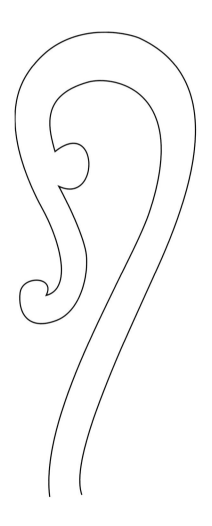

These blocks show how you can take an element from a sashing motif to create a block which will lend continuity to your quilt. Two different ways of using the motif in repetition are shown. Either of these blocks could be used in a traditional square block or in a round block. Also notice how the corner of the sashing had to be modified slightly in order to make the turn.

Hook, Line & Sinker

This sashing element is a variation on the previous element.

Here, I've used the sashing element to create a block.
Also, notice the corner modification in the border.

Feathered Hook

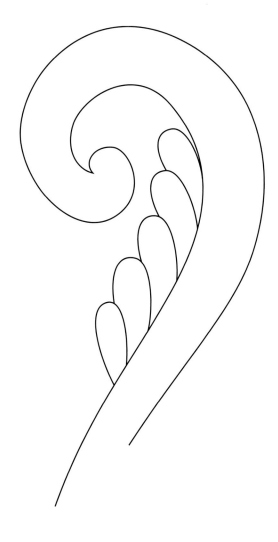

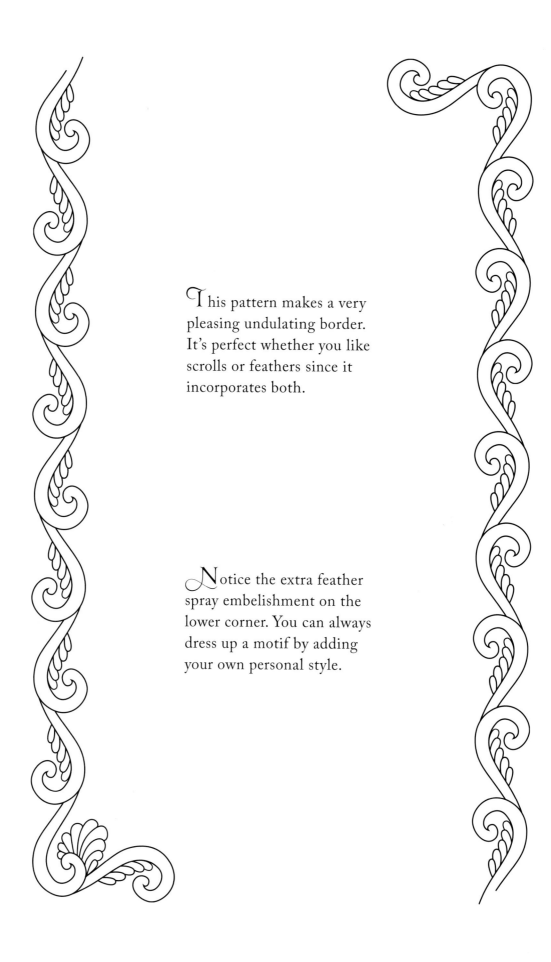

This pattern makes a very pleasing undulating border. It's perfect whether you like scrolls or feathers since it incorporates both.

Notice the extra feather spray embelishment on the lower corner. You can always dress up a motif by adding your own personal style.

Scroll & Fletching

Here are four more style options for the corners:

No feathers.   Feathers outside.   Feathers inside.   Feathers both sides.

Hook, Line & Fig Vine

Feel free to get creative with this sashing motif. Try out any of these block variations or make a leafy border. Add more leaves wherever you want. See how I added an additional leaf on the outside of the scroll at the corner?

Hook, Line & Floral

I loved the flowers in the sashing but they didn't seem to fit well in the blocks.

Boil, Toil & Tribal Scroll

This motif is made to be continuous. It is two, similar elements, joined and repeated. The corner has to be "nudged" a bit to make it work but once you are around the corner you can just keep on going. This pattern reminds me of a mountain road switchback.

Gargoyle Fire Scroll

Here's another example of drawing in part of a pattern and then reflecting and repeating to create the finished product. In this case, the border on the right.

$\mathcal{T}$his motif
makes some wild
looking blocks.

Wholecloth Pattern

This pattern took a bit of nudging to make it work and your creations might too. Keep trying, work with your space and don't get too frustrated. Your best work gets done by doing the hardest thing.

Karen's Final Thoughts

When making a decision to use curved crosshatching or straight crosshatching in a quilt, I always let the quilt top make the decision for me. I ask myself a few questions while looking at the quilt top:

1. Is this a traditional or non-traditional quilt? If the quilt top is non-traditional, with non-traditional fabrics, you can add a non-traditional spin to it by adding curved crosshatching.

2. Are the fabrics in the quilt too busy to handle crosshatching, causing the crosshatching to be lost or disappear completely, or is the print in the fabric plain enough to handle the crosshatching so all my work is noticeable?

3. Will my curved crosshatching appear elegant and enhance the quilt top, or will it appear disruptive to the piecing?

4. Will my curved crosshatching be enhanced if I use matching thread or contrasting thread?

Making a decision to use curved crosshatching or not, depends on the "busy-ness" of your quilt top fabric. You don't want your beautiful quilting to disappear in the busy fabric of the pieced top, so you will need some "plain space" fabric to show off your quilting. The quilts in this book feature curved crosshatching on plain fabric.

I would not recommend using a high contrasting thread unless it is a contemporary quilt. Also, unless you are fearless, or have excellent control of your machine, or you are a hand-quilter, I would not recommend using high contrasting threads at all since they will show every single mistake you make. I like to match my thread color to my fabric which hides many imperfections and mistakes along the way. No one likes to rip out stitches!

Each quilter prefers different methods of marking quilts or not marking quilts. I have always felt very comfortable marking my quilt tops and prefer to mark the quilt top. I enjoy the accuracy of that insurance. Ronda Beyer often does not mark her quilts. She simply plops down her *Ronda's Rulers* and quilts away with the no marking method.

This book and DVD show both methods, mark and no mark, to help you decide which method will work best for you. Whether you are a hand-quilter, use a home sewing machine, or quilt on a longarm quilting machine, you can achieve curved crosshatching. ✃

Karen's Bio

Longarm machine quilting allows Karen to combine her two passions: Wholecloth and Trapunto. Karen specializes in teaching and crafting award-winning quilts using techniques which allow machine quilters to replicate traditional "hand-quilted" effects. She has been featured on PBS's *Quilt Central* and HGTV's *Simply Quilts*. Her work has appeared in Joanne Line's books, *Quilts from the Quilt Makers Gift #1 and #2,* and numerous national magazines and journals. *Custom Curves* is Karen's fifth book. It is available, along with Karen's first four books, *Whitework Quilting, Mastering the Art of McTavishing, The Secrets of Elemental Quilting* and *Quilting for Show,* through www.onwordboundbooks.com and select retailers. Karen has supported her family as a full-time, professional longarm quilter since 1997, teaching McTavishing, Trapunto, Wholecloth Design and advanced longarm and domestic machine quilting workshops. Karen lives in Duluth, Minnesota on Lake Superior's North Shore, quilting and teaching throughout the country. ∾

Contact her:
Karen McTavish
McTavish Quilting Studio
Author, Speaker, Instructor, &
National Award Winning Quilter
2614 E. Superior Street
Duluth, MN 55812
Phone: 218-391-8218
Website: www.designerquilts.com
Email: kmctavish@designerquilts.com

Acknowledgements

Thanks to On-Word Bound Books for making another great book and DVD and for supporting me as an author once again. A special thanks to Fil-Tec for coming out with a thread that I fell in love with and a pre-wound bobbin that controls the tension. Thank you to APQS for making such great machines, which in turn, make me look really good. Thank you to Ann Tash for allowing me the use of her "Crazy Quilt" for the cover of this book, which I quilted for my niece. A very special thank you to Kathy McTavish, Myrna Ficken, Ronda K. Beyer and to all my friends and family who helped me get to this stage in my life. I am very grateful for the things I have learned from the art of quilting. ∾

Products and People in the Book

Contributing Quilter
Ronda K. Beyer

Ronda has been surrounded by quilts her entire life. Her Grandma always had a quilt in a frame. She learned to hand quilt as a teenager and she continued this as an at-home business until her kids started school. Ronda purchased her first longarm machine in 2005 and has won six Best of Show Ribbons at National Shows, two Viewers Choice ribbons, two Best Longarm Workmanship Ribbons, as well as many other prestigious ribbons. Along with her show work, she recently taped with Alex Anderson and Ricky Tims for *The Quilt Show* and taped with Karen McTavish for this book, *Custom Curves*, showcasing her method of curved crosshatching using her rulers, *Ronda's Rulers,* which are produced by Quilter's Rule. Ronda resides in Tualatin, Oregon but can often be found in her mom's quilt shop, Jane's Fabric Patch, in Tillamook, Oregon, which her mom started 30 years ago. Ronda has two children: her son who passed away in 2007 and her daughter who resides on the southern Oregon coast. She enjoys time with her grandson and three granddaughters when she is not quilting. ☙

Resources

Contact Ronda:
Ronda K. Beyer
8336 SW Tygh Loop
Tualatin, OR 97062
Phone: 503-956-8401
Email: rondakae@hotmail.com

To buy Ronda's Rulers:
Quilter's Rule International, LLC
817 Mohr Avenue
Waterford, WI 53185
Phone: 262-514-2000
Fax: 262-514-2100
Website: www.quiltersrule.com
Email: customerservice@quiltersrule.com

Longarm Quilting Contact:
American Professional Quilting Systems (APQS)
8033 University Ave. Suite F.
Des Moines, IA 50325
Phone: 515-267-1113 or 1-800-426-7233
Website: www.apqs.com

Recommended Thread and Bobbin:
Fil-Tec, Inc. ~ Bobbin Central
Glide polyester thread & Magna-Glide bobbins.
PO Box B
Hagerstown, MD 21741-1191
Phone: 1-800-258-5052
Fax: 1-301-824-6938
Website: www.bobbincentral.com

DVD Table of Contents

Problems with your DVD?

First, try playing your DVD on another DVD player or on your computer. Also, if you are playing your DVD on your computer, make sure you have a DVD drive, not just a CD drive. DVD's and CD's look the same but they are not. If you are having trouble getting the whole DVD to play in sequence on your DVD player, go back to the "main menu" on your DVD and highlight each chapter that you want to view. Not all DVD players will play the DVD from start to finish.

This DVD is designed to play from start to finish or in parts. To play a specific section, select the desired lesson from the main menu. This DVD has been formatted to play on NTSC machines in North America. NTSC formatting should work in newer DVD's and TV's from Europe, Australia, New Zealand and Asia as well. If you are from a country which supports PAL formatting, and you can't get the DVD to play, or it plays in black and white, try playing the DVD in your computer or on a newer DVD player with an NTSC compatible TV.

Write to us at contactus@onwordboundbooks.com and let us know if you are having a problem playing your DVD. We will work to resolve the problem and if your DVD is cracked or defective, we will replace it.